Original title:

The Blueprint of Love

Copyright © 2024 Book Fairy Publishing

Author: Juliet Astor
ISBN HARDBACK: 978-9916-87-255-0
ISBN PAPERBACK: 978-9916-87-256-7
ISBN EBOOK: 978-9916-87-257-4

A Journey in Union

In morning light, we set our sail,
Two hearts align, a whispered tale.
The wind will guide, the waves will speak,
Together strong, we are not meek.

Through valleys low, and mountains tall,
Hand in hand, we'll never fall.
With every step, a bond we weave,
In love and trust, we truly believe.

The stars will shine, our paths in sight,
In twilight's glow, we'll chase the night.
In laughter shared and silence kind,
A journey forged, our souls entwined.

When storms arise, we stand as one,
In trials faced, our hearts overcome.
With every turn, a story spun,
In union strong, our dreams begun.

Whispers of the Heart's Design

In quiet moments, secrets sigh,
Soft echoes dance beneath the sky.
A tapestry of dreams unfolds,
In whispered tones, the heart beholds.

Through gentle winds, our spirits sway,
Each glance a note in love's ballet.
Together woven, fate entwined,
In whispers true, our souls aligned.

Cartography of Affection

Across this map where feelings flow,
Each route a story, love's bright glow.
In valleys deep and mountains high,
Our hearts chart paths that never die.

With every step, a mark we lay,
A journey bright, come what may.
In every touch, a world expressed,
Cartography of love's true quest.

Threads of Connection

In every laugh, a thread is spun,
Binding hearts, two becoming one.
Through trials faced, the fabric tight,
A tapestry of shared delight.

In silence shared, a bond we weave,
In the simplest moments, we believe.
With fading light, our stories blend,
Threads of connection never end.

Architecture of Togetherness

With every brick, we build a space,
A sanctuary, love's embrace.
The walls adorned with memories bright,
In laughter's echoes, pure delight.

The roof above, a shelter strong,
In harmony, we both belong.
In every room, our dreams reside,
Architecture of hearts allied.

Whispers of a Shared Dream

In twilight's glow, we find our place,
A quiet sigh, a gentle trace.
With every heartbeat, tales unfold,
In whispered dreams, our hopes are bold.

Together, paths of light align,
In shadows cast, our spirits shine.
With trust as roots, we rise and soar,
Two souls entwined, forevermore.

Patterns Woven in Time

Under the stars, we weave the night,
Threads of stories, pure and bright.
Each moment holds a timeless grace,
In patterns made, we find our space.

With every stitch, our lives entwine,
In rhythmic beats, a song divine.
Through ebb and flow, we mark our days,
In woven threads, our love displays.

Threads of Togetherness

In golden fields, we dance along,
With laughter sweet, our hearts are strong.
Each thread a bond that we create,
In unity, we celebrate.

Through storms we stand, hand in hand,
Together forged, a mighty band.
In all we face, we share the load,
With threads of love, we share the road.

Crafting a Connection

With every word, a bridge we build,
In silence speaks the heart fulfilled.
Through every glance, a spark ignites,
In crafting bonds, we soar to heights.

In every laugh, a story grows,
With gentle hands, our love bestows.
Together now, we shape our way,
In crafted hearts, forever stay.

Building Bridges of Emotion

Across the rivers, feelings flow,
Connecting hearts in ebb and glow.
With every step, we share our fears,
Building bridges to dry our tears.

In whispers soft, our hopes combine,
Each moment crafted, pure, divine.
Together strong, we rise and stand,
With open hearts, we hold each hand.

Maps of Milestones

With pen in hand, we chart our fate,
Each little mark, a world we create.
Journeys taken, lessons learned,
In maps of milestones, wisdom earned.

Through valleys deep and mountains high,
We trace our steps beneath the sky.
Each path a story, rich and bright,
Guiding souls through day and night.

Designs of Desire

In shadows cast, our dreams take flight,
With every heartbeat, a spark ignites.
Blueprints drawn from passion's fire,
Creating worlds of pure desire.

The colors swirl, emotions rise,
Each stroke a glimpse of paradise.
In the canvas of our soul's embrace,
We find our truth in love's sweet grace.

A Symphony of Sentiments

In twilight's hush, the silence sings,
A harmony of gentle things.
Notes of laughter fill the air,
In every heartbeat, love laid bare.

Strings of hope weave through the night,
Each moment shared, a pure delight.
Together now, we rise and flow,
In this grand symphony, we glow.

The Rendering of Together

In sunlight's glow, we dance as one,
Paths entwined, our journey begun.
Laughter carries on the breeze,
Holding tight through gentle pleas.

Moments shared, the world is bright,
In your eyes, I find my light.
Hand in hand, we face the day,
With heartbeats that will always stay.

Stages of Inextricable Bonds

From seeds of trust, the roots will grow,
In fields of dreams, together we sow.
Through storms we stand, unyielding and strong,
In every note, we sing our song.

With every glance, a world is made,
In silent whispers, love won't fade.
Through every phase, we'll rise and fall,
Together, we will conquer all.

Heartstrings in Harmony

In the quiet night, your heartbeat sings,
A melody of love, the joy it brings.
With every touch, the music flows,
In perfect tune, the passion grows.

Strings entwined, a symphony bold,
In the warmth of arms, we break the cold.
Each note we play, a story told,
In love's embrace, we turn to gold.

Echoes of Affection

In the whispers of the twilight air,
Echoes linger; love is everywhere.
With every laugh, memories bloom,
Lighting dark corners of every room.

Through shadows cast, we find our way,
In every heartbeat, hope will stay.
Bound by grace, our spirits soar,
In echoes deep, we find much more.

Pathways to the Heart

In quiet whispers, secrets shared,
Two souls dance, their spirits bared.
Through winding roads, they find a way,
Love's gentle touch lights up the day.

Each step taken, hands entwined,
A journey drawn, two hearts aligned.
In laughter's echo, in silence' grace,
They carve their dreams in time and space.

Blueprints of Tenderness

With every line, a promise drawn,
A tender touch from dusk till dawn.
The plans we sketch in softest hues,
Speak of a bond that will not lose.

Through storms of life, our shelter stands,
Built on trust, with hopeful hands.
Each brick a memory, love the glue,
In the blueprint of me and you.

The Foundation of Us

Roots entwined beneath the ground,
In every glimpse, our love is found.
A sturdy base, we pave the way,
For dreams that blossom, day by day.

Together strong, we weather time,
Each heartbeat matches, in perfect rhyme.
With every trial, our bond will grow,
In the foundation of us, we know.

Etched in Each Other

In quiet moments, stories blend,
Our names are carved, a lifelong friend.
Memories linger, shadows cast,
Etched in each other, forever last.

In laughter's light and tear's embrace,
We find our truth, our sacred space.
Imprints of love, there we reside,
Etched in each other, side by side.

Harmonics of Hearts

In whispers soft, our souls collide,
Echoes dance where love resides.
Melodies weave through starry nights,
Creating bonds with gentle lights.

The rhythm sways, a sweet embrace,
Together we find our sacred space.
Each heartbeat sings a timeless tune,
Underneath the watchful moon.

Tapestry of Tenderness

Threads of kindness softly spun,
Weaving dreams from hearts as one.
Colors blend, a vibrant hue,
Stitching moments, old and new.

In woven patterns, love persists,
Through gentle touch and fleeting trysts.
Embroidered hopes in every seam,
Crafting life from shared esteem.

Blueprints of Belonging

Lines drawn clear with careful thought,
A place for all that love has sought.
Foundations strong in laughter's sound,
Roots intertwine, together bound.

Plans unfold beneath the sky,
Dreams constructed, reaching high.
In every brick, a story told,
A home built warm against the cold.

Schematics of Serenity

Calm waters reflect a tranquil mind,
In whispered breezes, peace we find.
Blueprints of stillness, laid with care,
A quiet heart in tranquil air.

Each line designed with purpose bright,
Guiding us through the soft twilight.
In the hush of moments shared,
Serenity blooms, always prepared.

Designs of Longing

In twilight whispers, dreams take flight,
A canvas woven, in soft moonlight.
Threads of hope, tied with care,
Silken shadows linger, love laid bare.

Each stitch a heartbeat, loud and clear,
A tapestry of wishes, drawing near.
Colors blend, in passion's glow,
The art of yearning, a delicate show.

Fields of memory, where hearts reside,
Echoes of laughter, where love confides.
Patterns unfold, in gentle grace,
Designs of longing, a warm embrace.

Patterns of Intimacy

Fingers entwined, a silent pact,
In the warmth of whispers, feelings exact.
Each glance exchanged, a language rare,
Crafting moments, with tender care.

Close in the shadows, secrets bloom,
Mapping connections, dispelling gloom.
Layers unfurl, revealing the soul,
Patterns of intimacy, making us whole.

In the hush of dusk, hearts collide,
Understanding woven, side by side.
Each thread a promise, steadfast and true,
Together we shine, in vivid hue.

The Fabric of Desire

In the weave of night, desires ignite,
Soft murmurs rise, a thrilling sight.
Textures whisper, soft and rough,
The fabric of longing, rich enough.

Fleeting moments, stitched in time,
Every heartbeat, a silent rhyme.
Intertwined souls, in passionate chase,
The fabric of desire, rapture's grace.

Embers glow, in the depth of eyes,
Threads of connection, a bold surprise.
Every glance, a spark that inspires,
In the tapestry woven, is love's desires.

Structures of Empathy

In the architecture of hearts, we stand,
Building bridges, hand in hand.
Listening closely, to every sigh,
Structures of empathy, we will never deny.

Foundations laid, with care and trust,
In every interaction, we find the must.
Walls of judgment, we gently break,
Strength in understanding, for compassion's sake.

Together we rise, in shared delight,
Embracing sorrows, bringing light.
In this design of human grace,
Structures of empathy, a warm embrace.

Fractals of Fidelity

In whispers of time, we entwine,
Echoes of love in every design.
A tapestry woven with threads of trust,
In the dance of our hearts, it's a must.

Reflections so bright in the mirror of souls,
Each promise we make, a story that rolls.
Layered together, like fractals unfold,
In patterns of warmth, our truths are told.

Through storms that may come, we stand hand in hand,
In the depths of our loyalty, forever we stand.
Each moment a fracture, yet beauty we find,
In the fractals of fidelity, our hearts aligned.

A Serenade to Togetherness

In the still of the night, our voices rise,
A melody sweet, beneath starlit skies.
Each note a reminder of the bond we share,
In the serenade of life, we find love's care.

Through valleys we walk, through mountains we climb,
Together in rhythm, we conquer all time.
With laughter and tears, our symphony sings,
In the harmony found, joy's spirit clings.

Hands held tight, we sway to the tune,
In gardens of dreams, we pluck each bloom.
A serenade woven, through thick and through thin,
Celebrating together, where love will begin.

The Poetry of Together

In every heart, a poem waits,
Written in silence, it reverberates.
With stanzas of hope and verses of grace,
Together we pen our unique embrace.

Where words may falter, our souls speak clear,
In the light of your gaze, I find no fear.
Each line, a promise, a journey we take,
The poetry of together in all that we make.

Through pages we turn and stories we share,
In the ink of our laughter, we lay ourselves bare.
The rhythm of life, a quill in our hand,
In the poetry of together, forever we stand.

Nesting Hearts

In branches entwined, our hearts find rest,
In the nest we've built, love feels the best.
With every gentle whisper, we lay our plans,
Nesting together, like soft grains of sand.

Through seasons that change, we weather the storms,
In the warmth of your embrace, my spirit transforms.
A sanctuary made from the love we've sown,
In the home of our hearts, we are never alone.

With each shared moment, we craft a nest,
In the softness of dawn, we are truly blessed.
Nesting hearts sheltered from the world outside,
In the cocoon of our love, forever we'll bide.

Stitching Moments Together

In the quiet dawn of day,
Threads of time weave and sway.
Moments stitched with care and grace,
In this tapestry, we find our place.

Memories blend, a gentle seam,
Each laugh and whisper, a shared dream.
Fingers dance on fabric bright,
Crafting love in morning light.

Every patch tells a story old,
In colors vibrant, warmth unfolds.
Through trials, joy, and bittersweet,
Together, our hearts skip a beat.

As nights fall softly, shadows play,
We gather moments, come what may.
Stitching time with every smile,
In our quilt, we walk each mile.

A Garden of Gestures

In a garden lush with hues,
Simple gestures bloom like dew.
A smile shared, a hand to hold,
In every act, a tale unfolds.

Sunlight kisses petals bright,
Kindness shines, a guiding light.
Soft whispers in the breeze,
Stirring hearts with gentle ease.

With every seed of love we plant,
The flowers of friendship enchant.
In this haven, dreams take root,
Sprouting joy, sweet and resolute.

As seasons change and petals fall,
Our garden thrives through it all.
Together we nurture and grow,
In this space, our love will show.

Elevations of Emotion

Heights we reach with every sigh,
Mountains of feeling, soaring high.
Emotions dance like clouds on air,
In every heartbeat, love laid bare.

Whispers echo in the night,
Stars illuminate our flight.
Through valleys low and skies so blue,
Together we find what feels so true.

With every pulse, our spirits rise,
Inflated dreams, we touch the skies.
In this journey, hand in hand,
Elevations where hearts expand.

Through storms that clash and winds that blow,
Our bond, a compass, helps us know.
In the realm of emotion, we find,
Elevated souls, forever entwined.

The Palette of Togetherness

With colors bright and shades so deep,
A palette woven, secrets to keep.
Each hue a story, rich and bold,
In the canvas of lives, love unfolds.

Brushstrokes dance in vivid light,
Creating dreams that take their flight.
Together we blend in harmony,
In this masterpiece, just you and me.

Layers of laughter, strokes of grace,
Paint our memories, time can't erase.
In this art, our spirits blend,
A vibrant tale with no end.

With every touch, our colors mix,
A symphony of joy, a heart's fix.
In the palette of togetherness,
Life's masterpiece, our happiness.

Palettes of Promise

In hues of dawn, the day unfolds,
Dreams painted bright with stories told.
Every shade whispers a new chance,
Life's vibrant dance, a swirling trance.

With every stroke, a tale begins,
Colors blend where hope never thins.
Brushes dipped in love's embrace,
Artistry blooms in every space.

Rainbows form from tears of joy,
Palette rich, a heart's own toy.
Future shines in every hue,
A promise born, forever true.

As twilight falls, the colors melt,
In silence, all the dreams are felt.
A canvas blank, yet filled with grace,
In every heart, a sacred place.

Structures of the Soul

Foundations deep, the heart will rise,
Crafted whispers beneath the skies.
Walls of hope built strong and high,
A shelter found when spirits fly.

In every crack, a story lives,
Bricks of memories, the heart gives.
Windows wide let laughter gleam,
Within these walls, we dare to dream.

In corridors of time we roam,
The echo of a cherished home.
Each structure tells of love's embrace,
Within these bounds, we find our space.

Through storms that howl, we stand secure,
Our inner strength, forever pure.
These structures hold, protect, and guide,
In the soul's depth, we will abide.

The Art of Embracing

With open arms, we greet the day,
In every moment, come what may.
Gentle touch, a feeling shared,
In warmth and comfort, we are spared.

The world can be both kind and cold,
Together, we can be so bold.
Embrace the light, the shadows too,
In each turn, discover something new.

Connections forged in laughter's glow,
In every heart, love's river flows.
Together held, through thick and thin,
The art of embracing lies within.

So take my hand, let spirits soar,
In unity, we can explore.
Through all the trials, we will stand,
In love's embrace, forever hand-in-hand.

Canvas of Connection

A tapestry of hearts entwined,
Colors merge, our souls aligned.
Each thread a story, carefully sewn,
On this canvas, we have grown.

Brushes dipped in laughter's light,
Creating sparks that shine so bright.
Together we weave a rich design,
In unity, our lives combine.

As seasons change, the patterns shift,
With every moment, a cherished gift.
In kindness shared, we find our way,
A masterpiece that will display.

On this canvas, we paint with love,
An artwork blessed from above.
Through every trial, joy will reign,
In this connection, none in vain.

Verses of Vulnerability

In shadows deep, we find our fears,
Whispers soft, of silent tears.
A fragile heart, exposed and raw,
Yearning for a gentle flaw.

A tender touch can heal the wound,
In honest light, true strength is found.
Embracing flaws, we learn to rise,
In vulnerability, freedom lies.

Merging Stars

Two distant lights that shine so bright,
Colliding paths in the still of night.
From cosmic dust, we weave our fate,
In the vastness, love can't wait.

As galaxies swirl, we dance and twirl,
To the song of the universe, we unfurl.
Each heartbeat echoes through the dark,
Together we ignite a spark.

The Heart's Compass

In moments lost, we seek the way,
A guiding force that won't betray.
Through trials faced and storms we weather,
Our hearts align, it leads us together.

Each choice we make, a step we take,
The compass turns, it's never fake.
With every breath, we find our ground,
In love's embrace, our truth is found.

Symmetry of Souls

Two halves that fit, a perfect whole,
In harmony, we find our goal.
Reflections deep in every glance,
A silent pact, a timeless dance.

Through struggles faced, we learn and grow,
The beauty found in ebb and flow.
In balance struck, we rise and soar,
In unity, forevermore.

The Geometry of Emotion

Lines of joy, curves of pain,
Angles sharp, love's sweet gain.
Shapes of longing, forms of bliss,
In this canvas, none we miss.

Circles close, yet far they stray,
Triangles whisper what hearts say.
In symmetry, our thoughts engage,
In this art, we turn the page.

Rectangles hold our hopes so true,
Polygons of me and you.
Each vertex tells a different tale,
In this structure, we prevail.

From patterns deep, we find our way,
Through light and shadow, night and day.
In every shape, emotions swell,
A geometry we know too well.

The Intersection of Dreams

At crossroads where our hopes align,
Paths converge, your hand in mine.
Whispers of tomorrows bright,
In the twilight, take your flight.

Turning corners, futures call,
In that moment, we stand tall.
Every dream, a guiding star,
Leading us to who we are.

Lanterns hung along the way,
Casting glow on paths we lay.
In the night, our visions blend,
A journey where the soul won't bend.

With every step, we weave the night,
In the dance of wrong and right.
Together, dreams are drawn anew,
At the intersection, me and you.

Keys to the Heart

Rusty locks and hidden doors,
Secrets held on whispered shores.
In this chest of old desires,
Lie the keys to endless fires.

Turn the lock and let it show,
What lay buried deep below.
In shadows cast, our spirits glow,
With every turn, our love will grow.

The silver key, it shines with grace,
Unlocking every hidden space.
With every twist, we share our art,
Crafting trust, the key to heart.

Gold and diamond, jeweled skies,
In this chamber, no goodbyes.
Together we will dare to start,
With the sacred keys to heart.

Mosaic of Heartbeats

Scattered pieces, bright and bold,
Crafting stories, love untold.
Each fragment tells of moments shared,
In this art, we are prepared.

Vivid colors mixed with pain,
Texture rich, a sweet refrain.
In the gaps, our laughter rings,
A patchwork quilt of heartfelt things.

Every heartbeat a unique thread,
Stitching memories that we've bred.
From broken shards, a beauty found,
In this mosaic, we stand our ground.

With every piece, we shape our fate,
In silent whispers, we create.
Together, as we find our way,
This mosaic brightens our day.

Lines of Devotion

In quiet whispers, hearts collide,
With every beat, love's gentle tide.
Through stormy nights and sunny days,
We find our truth in tender ways.

With every glance, a story told,
In every hug, a warmth to hold.
Together we weave, thread by thread,
A tapestry where dreams are fed.

In laughter shared, sorrows eased,
In moments small, our souls are pleased.
Each promise made, a sacred vow,
With each new dawn, we find our now.

Through the years, like vines we grow,
In every shadow, love's light will show.
Bound by the joys and pains we face,
In every heartbeat, we find our place.

Shaping Our Dreams

In realms of thought, we take our flight,
With courage bright, we chase the light.
Through doubts that cling, we bravely stand,
Together, we craft with gentle hands.

With every vision, a spark ignites,
Through sleepless nights, we scale new heights.
In every heart, potential glows,
As we embrace what passion sows.

The canvas wide, our colors blend,
With every stroke, our dreams ascend.
In unity, we rise and strive,
With love as fuel, our hopes revive.

Through trials faced, we carve our way,
In stormy seas, we learn to sway.
Each dream pursued, a step in dance,
In life's great play, we find our chance.

The Symphony of Us

In harmony, our spirits play,
Each note a bond that will not sway.
Together, we compose a tune,
Beneath the stars, or 'neath the moon.

With every laugh, a melody,
In silence shared, sweet symphony.
Our hearts create a world so vast,
With moments cherished, love amassed.

In rhythm's pulse, our lives entwined,
With whispers soft, our souls aligned.
Through every change, we find our song,
In every right, and in the wrong.

As echoes fade, new chords arise,
In every glance, a sweet surprise.
Together, we embrace the sound,
In life's grand concert, love is found.

Fragments of Forever

In fleeting moments, time stands still,
We capture laughs, love's gentle thrill.
With every breath, we seize a piece,
In every heartbeat, a sweet release.

The memories bloom, like flowers bright,
In shadows cast by fading light.
Though time may fade, and seasons change,
Our bond remains, forever strange.

Through distant echoes, whispers call,
In every stumble, we rise tall.
Each fragment held, a treasure true,
In life's mosaic, me and you.

As chapters close, new tales we find,
In every turn, our hearts aligned.
With every glance, we'll brave the storm,
For love endures, a world reborn.

The Orchestrated Heart

In the symphony of dreams, we soar,
Each note a wish, a silent score.
With every beat, our hopes take flight,
The orchestrated heart shines ever bright.

Melodies weave through the air,
Binding souls with tender care.
Every longing finds its place,
In this harmonious, warm embrace.

Rhythms pulse in the quiet night,
A dance of shadows, a glimpse of light.
Together we play this grand design,
In sync, our hearts forever align.

Through crescendos and gentle sighs,
We find our truth in the starry skies.
In the music, together we find,
A love that's endless, intertwined.

Anchors of Aspiration

On rocky shores, our dreams take root,
Anchored firm, resolute pursuit.
Through stormy seas and skies of gray,
Our aspirations guide the way.

With every wave, we stand as one,
Together rising with the sun.
Hope is a beacon, shining bright,
In the darkest depths, a guiding light.

Friendship's bond becomes our sail,
Navigating paths where others fail.
In trust, we find our steady ground,
Anchored in dreams, forever bound.

As tides may shift, we hold on tight,
With courage as our inner sight.
In unity, we chase the stars,
Anchors of aspiration, no matter how far.

Basslines in Bonding

Deep within the rhythm's core,
Basslines thrum, they call for more.
In every vibration, hearts align,
Creating bonds, so pure, divine.

The beat we share, a soulful sound,
In every moment, love is found.
Harmonized in perfect time,
Together, we create our rhyme.

Through highs and lows, we sway as one,
With every pulse, our fears undone.
In this dance, we intertwine,
Basslines of life in every line.

So let us groove through endless night,
With every touch, we feel the light.
In unity, our spirits soar,
With basslines that connect us more.

The Garden of Connections

In a garden where whispers bloom,
Connections grow, dispelling gloom.
With every seed, a story sown,
In vibrant colors, love is shown.

Each friendship blooms like flowers bright,
Nurtured by laughter, joy, delight.
Roots intertwine beneath the ground,
In this sanctuary, peace is found.

Through seasons change, we flourish still,
In the gentle warmth, we feel the thrill.
Gardens thrive with care and grace,
In connections made, we find our place.

So let us tend this sacred land,
With open hearts and caring hands.
In every corner, life reflects,
The beauty of our shared connections.

Portrait of Partnership

In the quiet glow of dawn, they rise,
Hand in hand, under sprawling skies.
With laughter, they paint their shared days,
In vibrant hues, in gentle ways.

Dreams whispered softly in the night,
They hold each other, spirits in flight.
Through storms and sun, their trust remains,
In every joy and all the pains.

With every challenge, stronger they grow,
A bond eternal that continues to flow.
In the garden of life, together they bloom,
In love's sweet embrace, they find their room.

Years will scatter like leaves in the breeze,
But their partnership's roots will never cease.
Together they'll journey, hand in hand,
In this portrait of love, so carefully planned.

Signposts of Sentiment

On winding roads where memories weave,
Each signpost stands, daring to believe.
Through laughter echoed and tears that fall,
They guide the heart, they answer the call.

A touch, a glance, they tell the tale,
Of moments shared, of winds that sail.
In the quiet whispers, the world fades away,
As time etches love in shades of gray.

Beneath the stars, where wishes are made,
They find their truth, unafraid and unfrayed.
With every landmark that life sets apart,
They navigate journeys, two souls, one heart.

And when the road bends, new paths unfold,
The signposts of love are forever bold.
In every journey, in every ascent,
A map of the heart, a sign of sentiment.

Patterns of the Heart

In a tapestry woven with threads of gold,
The patterns of love, in stories retold.
Each moment a stitch, each tear a design,
An intricate weave of your heart and mine.

Through laughter and sorrow, colors collide,
In shades of emotion, where secrets reside.
A quilt of our dreams, both humble and grand,
United in rhythms that fate has planned.

The fabric of time, it frays at the seam,
Yet we stitch our hopes into every dream.
With patience, we gather the pieces apart,
Creating a masterpiece, the work of the heart.

As the years pass gently, the patterns grow clear,
In the patterns of life, I hold you near.
Together we flourish, a blend of our art,
In the beautiful chaos, we craft our part.

Interwoven Paths

Two paths that cross in the morning light,
Destined to merge, to dance through the night.
With every step, a story unfolds,
An adventure begun, as fate gently molds.

As seasons change and shadows grow long,
Together they sing a harmonious song.
With laughter as fuel and dreams as their guide,
In the journey of life, they walk side by side.

Through valleys and mountains, hand in hand,
Creating a map of this wonderful land.
In each twist and turn, a lesson they learn,
In the heat of the moment, their passions burn.

No matter the distance, they stay ever close,
In the intertwining, a love they can boast.
As they travel the roads, with hearts open wide,
In the interwoven paths, they find their stride.

Maps of Mutual Growth

In lands where dreams can bloom,
With every step we dare to take,
We chart the paths of hope,
Creating maps for futures awake.

Together we will sow the seeds,
Tending roots in fertile ground,
A garden filled with vibrant deeds,
Where echoes of our love resound.

With each new dawn, we build anew,
Our visions merge, like sun and sky,
In unity, our strength will grow,
A tapestry of you and I.

Side by side through storms and sun,
We navigate the winds of change,
With every turn, our hearts will run,
Expanding realms that feel less strange.

Dances of Devotion

In twilight's soft and gentle glow,
We move as one, our spirits free,
With every step, our feelings flow,
A dance of love's sweet harmony.

Whispers in the night ignite,
The rhythm of our hearts combined,
In every glance, a spark of light,
A waltz that destiny designed.

Through melodies of laughter shared,
We twirl beneath the starry dome,
With each embrace, a love declared,
In this grand ballroom, we are home.

So let the music play its part,
I'll follow where the lead will go,
In every beat, we weave our art,
Two souls entwined, a lovely flow.

Pillars of Partnership

United strong, we stand as one,
With hands entwined like roots of trees,
We weather storms, we chase the sun,
In trust and love, we find our ease.

Each pillar forged from shared delight,
Supports the dreams we dare to share,
Together shining, bold and bright,
In every challenge, we're a pair.

As seasons change, our hearts align,
A fortress built on sacred ground,
In laughter's echo, love divine,
We're pillars firm, forever bound.

With every moment carved in time,
We lift each other to new heights,
In partnership, a perfect rhyme,
Our union leads to endless sights.

A Voyage Through Togetherness

Upon the sea of dreams, we sail,
With sails of hope and hearts aglow,
Through waves of time, we will prevail,
In tides of love, our journey flows.

As stars align, we chart the course,
An odyssey of trust and fate,
With every storm, we find our force,
Together we will navigate.

With laughter as our guiding star,
And memories like treasures found,
Through every wave, we've come so far,
In every heartbeat, love is crowned.

So let us voyage, hand in hand,
In every moment, cherish yet,
In shared adventures, we will stand,
On shores of dreams that we'll beget.

Dimensions of Affection

In whispers soft, we find our way,
Through shadows cast, in light of day.
Each heartbeat echoes, true and clear,
In this vast space, I hold you dear.

A tapestry of tender threads,
Where every word and gesture spreads.
With every glance, a story told,
In warmth and kindness, hearts unfold.

The layers deep, we dive within,
A world of trust where love begins.
In silent moments, silence speaks,
A bond that flourishes, love unique.

Together we will navigate,
Each twist and turn, embrace our fate.
In dimensions wide, our spirits blend,
A journey shared, on love we depend.

Layers of Love

Beneath the skimming surface bright,
A deeper current holds us tight.
In every glance, a hidden truth,
In every touch, we find our youth.

Like petals soft, in colors rare,
Each layer speaks of love laid bare.
A whisper here, a laugh or sigh,
In every layer, we learn to fly.

Through storms and sun, we stand as one,
A bond that shines like morning sun.
With every challenge, roots grow deep,
In layers of love, our souls will leap.

So let us journey, hand in hand,
Through every layer, we will stand.
With open hearts, and arms so wide,
In layers of love, we'll surely bide.

Frameworks of Fidelity

In sturdy frames, our trust is built,
With honesty that cannot wilt.
Each promise made, a brick in place,
In frameworks strong, we find our grace.

Through storms that test, and trials near,
In loyalty, we conquer fear.
With every vow, a safe embrace,
In steadfast bonds, we find our space.

The architecture of our days,
In faithful hearts, love's tapestry lays.
Each moment shared, a beam of light,
Through darkest hours, we shine so bright.

So let us craft, with every stone,
A fortress where our love is grown.
In frameworks true, our spirits soar,
With fidelity, forevermore.

Cadence of Companionship

In rhythm soft, our hearts align,
A melody that feels divine.
Each laugh a note, each sigh a phrase,
In cadence sweet, we weave our days.

Through every storm, we dance and twirl,
In each embrace, our dreams unfurl.
With every heartbeat, life's refrain,
In harmony, we break the chain.

Together stepping, side by side,
In this duet, we will abide.
With gentle whispers, love's own call,
In cadence shared, we'll never fall.

So let us sway, in time's embrace,
With every move, a sacred space.
In friendship deep, our spirits blend,
In cadence of companionship, love will never end.

Curves of Companionship

In laughter we find our gentle bends,
Through shadows of time, we navigate trends.
With hands intertwined, we weave our fate,
In the warmth of friendship, we celebrate.

In whispers shared beneath the stars,
We build our moments, erase the scars.
With every turn, a story unfolds,
Within the embrace, our truth grows bold.

The path may twist, and storms may rise,
Yet together we'll stand, under vast skies.
With a heart that listens, and dreams that soar,
In the curves of this bond, we are never war.

Through valleys low and peaks so high,
We cherish each breath, under the sky.
In every curve, our spirits align,
Companionship's art, divine and fine.

Color Palette of Passion

In hues of red, our hearts ignite,
From gentle blush to fierce delight.
A canvas painted in fervent dreams,
Echoing love in vibrant themes.

The golden rays of morning light,
Chase away shadows, warming the night.
In every stroke, a story sings,
Of moments cherished, and the joy it brings.

Deep purple whispers, secrets shared,
A bond that strengthens, unprepared.
With azure depths, our souls entwine,
In this palette, love's colors shine.

Each color blends, a masterpiece true,
In the gallery of us, I see you.
Passion's canvas, an endless art,
A vivid reminder of a beating heart.

Mosaic of Memories

Pieces of laughter, fragments of tears,
We gather our moments throughout the years.
In every glance, a memory shines,
Creating a mosaic that gently aligns.

From summer sunsets to winter's chill,
Each tile reflects a shared will.
With stories woven, bright and bold,
Our tapestry of life, a treasure untold.

In whispers of youth and dreams anew,
We craft our path, both old and true.
With every shard, a lesson we find,
In the art of living, beautifully combined.

A mosaic of memories, our hearts in sync,
Every piece a puzzle, a moment to link.
Together we build this vibrant array,
In the story of us, forever we stay.

The Fabric of Us

Woven threads of laughter and sighs,
In patterns stitched beneath the skies.
Each fabric tells a tale unique,
In the warmth of our bond, love speaks.

Colors embrace the texture of time,
In the loom of life, our hearts rhyme.
With every stitch, a memory to hold,
The fabric of us, a story unfold.

From the silken threads of dreams we weave,
Stronger together, we dare to believe.
In shadows and light, our tapestry grows,
Through the echoes of life, our fabric flows.

In layers rich, a journey so vast,
Woven with love, it will ever last.
The fabric of us, a beautiful trust,
In this woven embrace, we forever adjust.

Harmony in Hidden Spaces

In corners where shadows play,
Soft whispers dance and sway.
A melody of heartbeats sound,
In silence, love is found.

Beneath the flicker of the night,
Moments bloom, pure and bright.
Every glance a tender thread,
In the quiet, words unsaid.

Within the walls we gently build,
A sanctuary, hearts are filled.
Each secret shared, a fragrant rose,
In hidden spaces, love grows.

Together we weave our dreams,
In the stillness, hope redeems.
Through the maze of time and place,
We find our harmony, our grace.

Arches of Affection

Under arches, love cascades,
Light and laughter softly wades.
In every curve, a story flows,
A bond that blossomed, forever grows.

With every step, we learn to trust,
Building bridges, rise from dust.
In the embrace of painted skies,
Our hearts unite, the spirit flies.

Through trials faced, together stand,
Each heartbeat joins, a guiding hand.
In the echo of our joyful song,
Affection's arch, where we belong.

As shadows fade into the dawn,
We linger on, forever drawn.
In the arches, time stands still,
A tapestry of dream and will.

Resonance of Relationships

In the weave of lives entwined,
Echoes linger, souls aligned.
A symphony of heart and mind,
In resonance, love defined.

Through changes vast, we learn to grow,
In each story, a seed we sow.
The laughter shared, the tears we shed,
In every moment, love is spread.

When distance calls, and time is tough,
Our bond remains, enduring, rough.
In whispered thoughts and gentle sighs,
A melody beneath the skies.

Together we rise, together we fall,
In the music of life, we embrace it all.
Amidst the chaos, we find our way,
Resonance of love guides the day.

Footprints on Shared Ground

On the path where we have roamed,
Footprints mark the love we've grown.
In every step, a memory made,
In shared ground, our fears allayed.

Through the seasons, sun and rain,
Each footprint tells of joy and pain.
Hand in hand, we journey far,
Guided by our inner star.

From whispered dreams to laughter bright,
We carve our truth in day and night.
On this soil, our hopes employed,
In the journey, love's deployed.

With every stride, together we stand,
Leaving traces in soft, warm sand.
In our hearts, we hear the sound,
Of love's journey on shared ground.

Cherished Coordinates

In the quiet of our shared space,
Lies the compass of your embrace.
Each heartbeat maps the way we roam,
Together, we craft a place called home.

Stars align in the midnight sky,
Guiding us, as we dare to fly.
With every step, a footprint stays,
Navigating love's endless maze.

Mountains tall and valleys low,
On this journey, our spirits grow.
With cherished coordinates, we define,
A world where yours forever aligns with mine.

So we'll wander, hand in hand,
Across this vast, enchanted land.
Every moment a map we weave,
In cherished coordinates, we believe.

Conducting the Heart's Melody

In twilight's glow, our hearts conspire,
Striking chords of deep desire.
With every note, our souls take flight,
Conducting love beneath the night.

Your laughter rings like silver chimes,
Echoing through my favorite rhymes.
Each whisper soft, a gentle caress,
Melodies blend, our souls compress.

Together we sway, a graceful dance,
In rhythm, we find our second chance.
With every heartbeat, a symphony plays,
Conducting dreams in endless rays.

So let us sing, side by side,
With love as our unwavering guide.
In harmonious union, forever we'll be,
Conducting the heart's sweet melody.

Illumination of Intertwined Souls

In shadows deep, our spirits glow,
Illuminating paths we know.
With every touch, we spark a flame,
Intertwined souls, forever the same.

Whispers linger in the night air,
Binding us close, a loving prayer.
In twilight's dance, we softly sway,
A beacon of light, we find our way.

Through silent storms and gentle rains,
Our love's a light that never wanes.
Illumination through joy and pain,
In intertwined souls, we gain a refrain.

Together we shine, two stars aligned,
In the universe, our love defined.
With every heartbeat, a bright, sweet toll,
In the illumination of intertwined souls.

The Map of Mutuality

In the sketch of life, we find our way,
Lines of friendship guide each day.
With open hearts and hands held tight,
We pave the way, igniting light.

Trust is the ink that writes our fate,
In mutuality, we cultivate.
Paths converge as we walk this line,
In moments shared, our hearts align.

From laughter shared to tears that flow,
Every chapter helps us grow.
The map of mutuality unfolds,
A treasure trove of stories told.

So let us chart our course ahead,
With love as our compass, by it we're led.
Together, always, through each endeavor,
In the map of mutuality, forever.

Parallels of Heartstrings

In the silence where dreams reside,
Two souls whisper, side by side.
Tangled threads of fate align,
In this dance, your heartbeat's mine.

Through valleys deep, and skies so wide,
We find our truth, we cannot hide.
Each step forward, hand in hand,
Our love blooms in this sacred land.

Mirrored thoughts in every glance,
In parallel paths, we find our chance.
With every trial, we grow together,
Like intertwined vines, we brace the weather.

So let the world, with all its noise,
Bear witness to our hearts' true choice.
For in this rhythm, pure and bold,
Is a story of love yet untold.

The Profile of Us

Captured shadows in twilight's glow,
Sketches of laughter, soft and slow.
In every curve, memories trace,
The vibrant contours of our space.

Through moments shared, the colors blend,
Each stroke a message we transcend.
In the gallery of dreams we build,
The essence of us, softly filled.

From candid smiles to dreams unknown,
Every heartbeat, a seed we've sown.
With each frame, our truth stands tall,
A masterpiece, our love's great call.

So here's our profile, forever drawn,
In a canvas where dusk meets dawn.
Every layer, a story spun,
A beautiful tale; we are just begun.

Elements of Affection

In the chaos of everyday life,
Your laughter cuts through like a knife.
Gentle breezes that whisper sweet,
In the dance of love, our hearts beat.

With every touch, we spark a flame,
A chemistry that feels the same.
Like fire and water, earth and air,
Our elements combine, a perfect pair.

Through storms and sunshine, we're entwined,
In every moment, love defined.
With every glance, we understand,
The heartbeat of this timeless strand.

Let the world observe and sigh,
For in our love, the elements fly.
Bound by nature's force and grace,
We find our place in this vast space.

Crafting Our Narrative

With ink and dreams, we pen our tale,
In chapters written, we shall prevail.
Each word a whisper, bold and bright,
Crafting our story, day and night.

From pages blank, our journey starts,
With every twist, we mend our hearts.
Through trials faced and joy reclaimed,
Our narrative's sung, forever named.

We meet the dawn with hope anew,
In every sunset, a love so true.
Together, we weave the fabric tight,
In the tapestry of day and night.

So let us write with passion's fire,
A story rich, that won't expire.
For in our words, the world will see,
The beautiful saga of you and me.

The Landscape of Emotion

In valleys deep, where sorrow lays,
Joy blooms bright in sunlit rays.
Each mountain high tells tales of fears,
Rivers flow, mixed with our tears.

The winds carry whispers of long-lost dreams,
Through fields of hope, where laughter gleams.
Rain provides life to the soul's dry ground,
In nature's embrace, solace is found.

Seasons change, with colors ablaze,
Capture moments in a warm haze.
The landscape shifts, yet emotions stay,
A canvas vast, where hearts freely play.

In shadows cast, we learn to grow,
Navigating paths with ebb and flow.
The landscape of feelings forever we roam,
In every heartbeat, we find our home.

Tapestry of Two

Threads of gold and threads of gray,
Woven tight in a dance each day.
Every stitch holds a secret tight,
In the warmth of love, we find our light.

Patterns formed in laughter's glow,
With quiet hugs, our spirits flow.
Each color sings a story rare,
A rich tapestry spun with care.

The frays remind us of moments tough,
Yet in the weave, we find enough.
Together we mend, together we strive,
In this fabric of life, we truly thrive.

Two hearts entwined, embracing the weave,
In the artistry of love, we believe.
Side by side, through storm and sun,
A tapestry of two, forever one.

Cornerstones of Companionship

Upon this ground, we lay our stones,
Each one whispers of the love we've grown.
With laughter built from countless days,
In every corner, memory stays.

The pillars strong, they stand so tall,
Together we rise, together we fall.
Through trials faced, our bond has sealed,
With every scar, a strength revealed.

Foundations laid in trust and care,
A sanctuary built, two hearts laid bare.
In moments shared, our spirits blend,
A testament to the love we send.

With every brick, we nurture dreams,
Forging a path, or so it seems.
Cornerstones strong, of faith and grace,
In companionship, we find our place.

Arches of Understanding

Beneath the arches, our voices meet,
Echoes of thoughts in a gentle beat.
Every bridge built on trust and time,
In every pause, a rhythm sublime.

We walk together on this grand span,
Hand in hand, as only we can.
Thoughts intertwined in a dance so rare,
In silence shared, our hearts lay bare.

The arches bend but do not break,
In the storms of life, new strength we make.
Each step forward, a promise finds,
In the depth of connection, true love binds.

Through every arch, we learn to see,
The beauty in you, reflected in me.
Together we rise, as skies expand,
Building bridges, hand in hand.

Sculpted by Serendipity

In gentle winds our paths collide,
With stars above as our guide.
Each twist and turn a chance to see,
Life's art, a grand serendipity.

Moments crafted in a dance,
Fate steps in, grants us a chance.
Whispers echo, hearts aligned,
In the magic of the kind.

We wander through this destined flow,
Where rivers of fortune freely go.
With every heartbeat, we explore,
A sculpture rich with tales of lore.

Through laughter, tears, and shared delight,
We shape our dreams, from day to night.
Sculpted by the hands of fate,
Together, we create, not wait.

Choreographed in Care

In quiet steps, we find our place,
A dance of love, a warm embrace.
With every glance, a silent cue,
Choreographed in shades of blue.

The rhythm soft, yet loud and clear,
Every heartbeat drawn near.
In harmony, we take the floor,
Expressing feelings, wanting more.

With grace we twirl, with strength we hold,
Stories of dreams in movements bold.
Our souls entwined, a timeless art,
Choreographed, we beat as one heart.

In every lift, a promise made,
A love that won't ever fade.
Together we dance through the night,
In the warmth of shared light.

The Architecture of Us

Brick by brick, we build our dreams,
In the sunlight's warmest beams.
Foundations deep, our roots entwined,
In every corner, love designed.

Walls adorned with memories sweet,
Each room a story, a heartbeat.
The windows wide, to let love in,
Architecture shaped from within.

The roof above, a shelter strong,
In storms we find where we belong.
With laughter's echo through the halls,
Construction thrives when love calls.

Together we sketch a future bright,
In every shade, in every light.
The architecture of our ties,
A masterpiece beneath the skies.

Foundations of Forever

In silent whispers, roots run deep,
Through trials faced, and promises we keep.
The ground we stand on, firm and true,
Foundations laid, me and you.

With time, we build, brick by brick,
Through storms and sunshine, thick and slick.
Conversations soft, a sturdy wall,
In the heart's keep, we stand tall.

Through every season, strong we grow,
In love's embrace, together we flow.
With warmth we gather, side by side,
In this sanctuary, we can abide.

Forever starts with every day,
In little acts, in what we say.
Together we forge this sacred ground,
In love's embrace, we are found.

Skylines of Sentiments

Beneath the twilight glow, we stand,
Dreams reflecting in the sand.
Whispers of the night take flight,
Painting stories in the light.

Mirrored in the city's haze,
Our laughter flows through winding ways.
Stars above in silent sync,
Guard our secrets, words unsaid, we think.

With every step, the world unfolds,
Memories formed, stories told.
Hand in hand, through highs and lows,
In this skyline, our love grows.

As twilight fades into the blue,
I find my home in you, it's true.
Each light a promise, a new start,
Our history lights up the heart.

A Flowing River of Us

In the heart of the forest deep,
Lives a river, secrets to keep.
Gentle currents, soft and sweet,
Where our souls are bound to meet.

Time meanders, to and fro,
Reflecting all the love we know.
Pebbles whisper, waters sing,
In this flow, we find our spring.

Beneath the branches, shadows play,
Guiding us on this wondrous way.
Together we drift, carefree and bold,
In this river, our stories unfold.

With every bend, new dreams await,
Carried forth by love's own fate.
As ripples dance in twilight's hue,
I find forever, my heart in you.

Cartography of Care

Drawn on paper, the lines we trace,
Mapping out our sacred space.
With every mark, a memory made,
In this cartography, never to fade.

From mountain peaks to valleys low,
Our journey a river, in gentle flow.
Every path, a choice we take,
In this landscape, bonds we make.

Light explodes in colors bright,
Guiding us through day and night.
Each dot a moment, perfectly placed,
A tapestry of love interlaced.

With compass in hand, we explore anew,
Every mile sings of me and you.
In the map of life, we find our way,
Woven together, come what may.

Seeds of Serendipity

Amidst the blossoms, hope takes root,
In gardens wild, we find the fruit.
Each moment sown with care and grace,
Sprouts of joy in every space.

Whispers carried on the breeze,
Timing's magic among the trees.
In tangled paths, we chance to meet,
Life's sweet dance on nimble feet.

As seasons shift and colors fade,
We find new roots in love displayed.
Every chance a treasure trove,
In this garden, our hearts rove.

Together we plant what's meant to be,
In the soil of sweet serendipity.
With every bloom, a story shared,
In this tapestry, all is bared.

The Map of Our Embrace

In twilight's glow, we trace the lines,
A compass drawn where heart defines.
With whispers soft, our futures chart,
Each fold and crease, a work of art.

Through valleys deep, and mountains high,
We navigate beneath the sky.
In laughter loud, and silence sweet,
Together still, we find our beat.

Our fingers touch, the ink runs warm,
Creating paths from every storm.
In every breath, our legends weave,
With hope and love, we shall believe.

So hand in hand, we roam this place,
Exploring love's eternal space.
We're maps alive, through time and dreams,
In every glance, a world redeems.

Sketches of Souls Entwined

Two hearts sketch dreams on paper thin,
With colors bright, where love begins.
A brush of fate, as shadows dance,
Creating art with every glance.

In twilight's hues, our stories blend,
Each curve and line, a love to mend.
With gentle strokes, we call it fate,
A portrait built, it can't wait.

Through tangled roots and swirling skies,
We paint our truth, and never lie.
With every shade, our passions rise,
In vibrant whispers, love replies.

So let us draw, with every breath,
In sketches sweet, we conquer death.
For life's a canvas, we engrave,
With sketches bold, our souls we save.

Framework of Passion

In twilight's grasp, a frame is drawn,
With beams of light, from dusk to dawn.
Each structure built, with trust and care,
Our passions rise, a bond to share.

Through storms we face, and sunlit days,
We strengthen walls in love's embrace.
With every level, our hearts align,
Constructing joy, our love divine.

Blueprints sketched with dreams in mind,
Each moment lived, forever twined.
In every heartbeat, nails and wood,
We frame our lives, as only we could.

Together forged, an unbroken trust,
In this framework, love is a must.
So let's build high, and never fall,
A passion's home, our one true hall.

Mosaic of Shared Moments

In fragments bright, our moments gleam,
A mosaic formed from love's great dream.
Each piece a tale, of joy and pain,
Together stitched, through sun and rain.

With varied hues and textures rare,
We weave a story beyond compare.
Each laugh, each tear, a tile in place,
Creating images time can't erase.

In every glance, a sparkle shines,
A patchwork made of heart's designs.
Together forged, in time's embrace,
Our life's mosaic, a sacred space.

So let us gather, as moments flow,
In every piece, our love will grow.
A tapestry of what we share,
In this mosaic, forever there.